JOURNEY TO SUCCESS

From the best-selling author of:

HOW TO GET **APPROVED** FOR

THE BEST MORTGAGE

WITHOUT STICKING A FORK IN YOUR EYE ™

Praise for Elysia Stobbe #1 Best Selling Author

"Five Stars. So awesome! Breaks it down for you without the confusion!"
– Karen Mahoy

"Just a wonderful read and very easy to understand. Seriously this is the only book you need. Just a wonderful read and very easy to understand. She knows her stuff."

"Coffee Table Must! As a novice in this area, I love having the pertinent information so clearly explained. A wonderful resource!"

"Thank you so much for breaking it down. I don't know what took me so long in purchasing this book, but I am glad I have it now. Thank you again."
– Dr. George Alden

Reviews

5.0 out of 5 stars
Awesome!
Reviewed in the United States on March 21, 2018
Verified Purchase
"This book was a great read, a must for all serious buyers and sellers. Deep wealth of information, helps to provoke your thinking and decision making."

5.0 out of 5 stars
Like having a personal Realtor speaking to you.
Reviewed in the United States on July 15, 2019
Verified Purchase
"This book clarified a lot of concerns I had with purchasing a home. After reading this book I feel much more confident about buying a home. Very easy read and easy to understand. When I emailed the author regarding my circumstances she quickly replied and even gave me a call to give me peace of mind. Highly recommend to anyone looking to buy a home."

inkedpaige
5.0 out of 5 stars
A confusing process made simple.
Reviewed in the United States on June 27, 2015
"I have been on a house hunt for about a year now and I've just been too scared to make the plunge. I didn't understand the process and it was overwhelming and intimidating. This book broke it down so easily!!! I highly recommend snagging a copy. Now I feel confident enough to go through with my dreams"

Phillip Stutts
5.0 out of 5 stars
Best mortgage book I've ever read.
Reviewed in the United States on September 18, 2015
"I found this book incredibly helpful and beneficial. Frankly, it's the best mortgage book I've ever read and I own many properties. Definitely worth the buy."

Elysia Stobbe

The essential Guide to **Jumpstart** your life by conquering doubt and
uncertainty to find peace plus **Prosperity** in a tumultuous world.

52 WEEKLY HABITS
YOU CAN MASTER

JOURNEY
TO
SUCCESS

WITHOUT STICKING A FORK
IN YOUR EYE™

ELYSIA STOBBE

Ponto Alto PUBLISHING

This book is for informational purposes; it is not intended to provide psychological, emotional, physical, spiritual or financial advice.

Ponto Alto Publishing
1001 Mayport Road, #331095
Atlantic Beach, FL 32233

First Ponto Alto Publishing softcover edition January 2021

For information about special discounts for bulk purchases, please contact Ponto Alto Publishing Special Sales at elysia@elysiastobbeinc.com

To contact Elysia Stobbe about speaking at your live event, email elysia@elysiastobbeinc.com

Manufactured in the United States of America

ISBN 978-0-9861620-2-2

Book design by: Brad Kuhn, brad@bradkuhnandassociates.com

Preface

Wow, what a year it has been! If your past year was challenging and you're ready for something new, this book is for you!

If you made lemons out of lemonade and want even more joy juice in your life, this book is for you! If you are successful and want even more fulfillment in your life, you've got the right book!

Have you ever felt stuck? Are you struggling to feel happiness and fulfillment? Or do you feel like you're just not where you "should" be or where you want to be on the path of life? The bottom line is that you can design your day, or you can let it run over you like a truck. The choice is yours.

Often what's holding us back from achieving what we truly want is self-perspective and the tools to implement what you've learned.

I've designed this book to be thought provoking and inspiring so that you can live the life of your own design and creation.

This book gives you the motivation and tools to build consistent skills that empower you to be your best self.

It is a weekly guide that enables you step by step to focus on your goals and what is actually important to you. Invest just a few minutes a week, and you will stay on your Journey To Success for the whole year.

If you would like your FREE Journey To Success Roadmap from Zero to Hero, visit: **KeyToSuccessInLife.com**

To get your best results and make an immediate impact in your life, grab the guided video course here: **WeeklySuccessHabits.com**

It's important to know your best assets and how they serve you. What are your best assets? Who are your best assets?

One trait that millionaires have in common is that they have multiple streams of income. If you are interested in learning about passive income and you want to focus on financial goals, go to: **FinancialFreedomStar.com**

For more about me, check out **ElysiaStobbeInc.com** as well as my other books at **ElysiaStobbeBooks.com**

I believe that we need motivation, gratitude, self-reflection and direction to achieve our goals. I'm a big believer in "I get to," instead of "I have to." I apply this to both my work and my personal life. This helps to reduce my stress level while letting me be present in my daily life instead of worrying about all the other things I "have" to get done.

Here are a few high level tips that I live by:

- Meditate each morning

- Focus on your outcomes

- Have clear, measurable goals and review them weekly

- Be proactive, not reactive

- Elysia Stobbe, December 28th, 2020

BE YOU   **DO YOU**   **FOR YOU**

Acknowledgments

Thank you to my Mama, Terry DeArmas, who told me when I was young, "Do what you want and the money will follow." I heard this from a young age and took it to heart. It is because of this I have always thought I could achieve whatever I wanted in my life. I have always followed my dreams and been fortunate through hard work to be financially successful as well as emotionally fulfilled. I am so grateful to live an amazing life!

Thank you to my family, friends, co-workers and clients. You inspire me, challenge me and make me laugh everyday. It is a privilege to serve you. You brighten my life and help me grow in so many wonderful ways.

Supreme gratitude to my best friends Kristine Kennedy, Marisha Chilcott and Tiffany Vasseur for their wonderful, supportive friendships. You accept me unconditionally and love me at my best and my worst. You are priceless to me, and I am so grateful to have you in my life.

Special thanks to Gregory Alexander who did an amazing job editing this book! Greg, I cherish our twenty-year friendship. Greg Alexander is an accomplished freelance writer and editor with over 25 years of experience. He is also an author of five books. https://gregoryjalexander.myportfolio.com

Thank you to Deborah Battersby, who helped me brainstorm the initial concept that became this book.

Thank you to Rudy Rodriquez who so beautifully reminds me of my worth (yes, I am human too, just like you) and inspires me to greater heights.

Thank you to Tony Robbins, who has positively changed my life forever.

Contents

Introduction

Who is this book for? This book is for people who want more out of life: more joy, more money, more happiness, more energy, more quality time with those you love and a better overall quality of life. This book is for people who want to become multimillionaires. This book is for people who want help with achieving their goals. This book is for people who want to retire early. This book is for people who can use a little extra nudge. This book is for people who want more focus. This book is for people who need guidance and direction. I believe we are always a work in progress, joyfully perfecting our own Journey To Success of who we are as individual human beings.

In my experience I have found that you become who you spend time with. So, choose your friends carefully and wisely. Take a look around you and see who you have surrounded yourself with. Because ultimately, for better or worse, that is who you will become.

Why me? I have a verifiable track record of success writing published articles on the topic of goal planning and goal setting. I have spoken at Harvard University twice and shared my own "Secrets of Success" and keys to "Managing Yourself & Leading Others". I am a Pulitzer Prize nominated and #1 Best Selling Author! I have been financially free for years. I routinely volunteer months of my time and money to various organizations and charities that are important to me. I have true work life balance and love my life!

I coach professionals to exceed their goals and make more money in their businesses while achieving a positive work life balance. There is nothing more rewarding to me than helping ordinary people achieve extraordinary results!

Why now? The idea for this book came to me several years ago. But I didn't take action until now. I believe now more than ever that we need direction and focus in our ever changing tumultuous world. Over the past year I've overcome many serious challenges, including health, isolation and financial. I've worked hard in my life to create and recently to recreate my successes. Over the past few years I developed these strategies of self-awareness and growth that will show you how to achieve various types of successes in your life.

What happens in a quarantine doesn't have to stay in quarantine. I'm excited to share this unique Journey To Success guide with you, so you can master your own universe!

How can you get the most out of this book? There is a chapter for each week of the year. Each one has a different focus—an inspirational, motivational or thought-provoking quote. Set aside a few minutes in a quiet place where you can concentrate, read the quote and see how it impacts you. How do you feel? What comes to mind? How does it resonate with you? Where does it show up in your life? What do you feel inspired to do differently? How can you make a change?

If you would like your FREE Journey To Success Quick Planning Worksheet with your quick start video guide, visit: **KeyToSuccessInLife.com**

To get the most out of this book, grab the weekly video guide here: **WeeklySuccessHabits.com**

I invite you to give this gift to yourself. Take this time for you every week and make this practice a weekly habit.

Of course, if you are already an overachiever, go ahead and read more than one a week. You can do so and then start over again in the middle of the year! You'll have a fresh perspective the second and third time around whether that's this year or next year.

I hope you enjoy my book and put it to good use to be your best self. Cheers! To your Journey To Success!

GRATITUDE

"Gratitude is a quality similar to electricity: It must be produced and discharged and used up in order to exist at all."

~ William Faulkner

Focus on *Gratitude*

Who makes you smile?

_____

_____

_____

_____

_____

_____

Who gives you great advice?

_____

_____

_____

_____

_____

_____

Are there little things you take for granted?

_____

_____

_____

_____

_____

_____

Who believed in you when you didn't?

_____
_____
_____
_____
_____
_____

Who has been generous to you?

_____
_____
_____
_____
_____

Who has taught you life lessons?

_____
_____
_____
_____
_____

Focus on *Gratitude*

What makes you laugh?

_____
_____
_____
_____
_____
_____

Who is supportive of you?

_____
_____
_____
_____
_____
_____

Who inspires you?

_____
_____
_____
_____
_____
_____

Who are you fortunate to have in your life?

_____
_____
_____
_____
_____
_____
_____
_____
_____

Who do you have wonderful memories of?

_____
_____
_____
_____
_____
_____
_____
_____
_____

Focus on *Gratitude*

What unique talents were you born with?

_____

_____

_____

_____

_____

_____

_____

_____

_____

What special skills have you developed?

_____

_____

_____

_____

_____

_____

_____

_____

_____

What are some of your greatest adventures?

_____

_____

_____

_____

_____

_____

_____

_____

_____

_____

_____

_____

_____

_____

_____

_____

_____

_____

_____

_____

_____

_____

Notes

YOU ARE UNIQUE

WEEK 2

"Here's to the crazy ones, the misfits, the rebels, the troublemakers, the round pegs in the square holes ... the ones who see things differently—they're not fond of rules, and they have no respect for the status quo. ... You can quote them, disagree with them, glorify or vilify them, but the only thing you can't do is ignore them because they change things. ... They push the human race forward, and while some may see them as the crazy ones, we see genius, because the people who are crazy enough to think that they can change the world, are the ones who do."

~ Steve Jobs

You are *Unique!*

Often we don't take the time to appreciate ourselves. We are each unique in our own special way. What's amazing about you?

_____

_____

_____

_____

_____

_____

_____

_____

_____

_____

_____

_____

_____

_____

_____

_____

_____

_____

_____

_____

_____

_____

_____

_____

_____

_____

_____

_____

_____

_____

_____

_____

_____

_____

_____

_____

_____

_____

_____

_____

_____

_____

_____

_____

Notes

MOMENTUM

WEEK 3

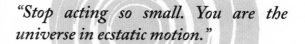

"Stop acting so small. You are the universe in ecstatic motion."

~ Rumi

Focus on *Momentum*

When you take action, each step (big or small) helps build momentum. Wherever you are in your journey, take action today. What can you do to keep your momentum toward your goals?

1. _____

_____

2. _____

_____

3. _____

_____

4. _____

_____

5. _____

_____

List the key steps needed to reach your ultimate goal for this year.

1. _____

_____

2. _____

_____

3. _____

_____

4. _____

_____

5. _____

_____

Celebrate your successes and reward yourself along the way.

Notes

WHAT IS STOPPING YOU?

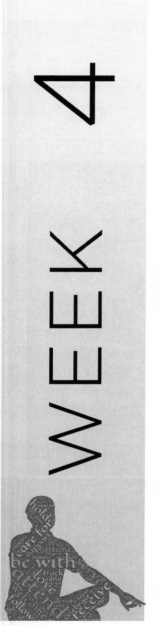

WEEK 4

"I learned the things you do not say seem to scream the loudest within."

~ Beau Taplin

Focus on getting *Unstuck!*

What holds you back? Why does it hold you back?

_____

_____

_____

_____

_____

_____

_____

_____

_____

Where do you feel stuck? When does this happen most often? What can you do to change that?

_____

_____

_____

_____

_____

_____

_____

_____

_____

What do you think or feel is keeping you from your goals?

_____

_____

_____

_____

_____

_____

_____

_____

_____

Why do you let that stop you? What can you do to change that behavior right now?

_____

_____

_____

_____

_____

_____

_____

_____

Notes

_____
_____
_____
_____
_____
_____
_____
_____
_____
_____
_____
_____
_____
_____
_____
_____
_____
_____
_____
_____

MASTER YOUR EMOTIONS

WEEK 5

"*I don't want to be at the mercy of my emotions. I want to use them, to enjoy them, and to dominate them.*"

~ Oscar Wilde

Focus on *Emotions*

When do you feel your best? Is it a certain time of day? Is it when you complete a task? Is it when you feel successful? Is it when you feel loved? Is it when you are doing a certain activity? Is it when you exercise? Is it in a certain place? Do all of these examples apply? Write your own details of when you feel your best.

_____

_____

_____

_____

_____

_____

_____

_____

_____

_____

_____

_____

Notes

SURROUND YOURSELF
WITH BEAUTY

"Whenever you are creating beauty around you, you are restoring your own soul."

~ Alice Walker

Focus on *Beauty*

*Our environment makes a difference.
What and who we surround ourselves with
contributes to our life, positively or negatively.
Pick three things you will surround yourself
with that make you feel good.*

_____

_____

_____

_____

_____

_____

_____

_____

_____

_____

_____

_____

_____

_____

_____

_____

_____

_____

_____

_____

_____

_____

_____

_____

_____

_____

_____

_____

_____

_____

_____

_____

_____

_____

_____

_____

Notes

EXECUTE

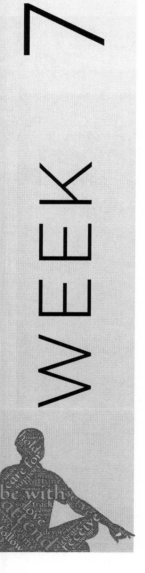

WEEK 7

"Vision without execution is delusion."

~ Thomas Edison

Focus on *Execution*

The best plans don't happen unless you actually do them. Yes, that's right, you actually have to do the work!

I do use hacks, shortcuts and leverage whenever possible. However, there are certain activities that I need to do to build myself as a human and grow my businesses.

My coaching clients know that in order to grow their business, they must complete income producing activities every day. Get clear on what you need to do daily to make your dreams happen and list them here.

These are three things I will do every week for my personal growth:

_____

_____

_____

_____

_____

_____

_____

_____

These are three things I will do every week for my business:

_____

_____

_____

_____

These are three things I will do each morning for my family:

_____

_____

_____

_____

Notes

COURAGE

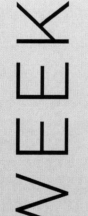

*"Success is not final, failure is not fatal:
it is the courage to continue that counts."*

~ Winston Churchill

Focus on *Courage*

What has happened to you that you didn't anticipate?

_____
_____
_____
_____
_____
_____
_____
_____

How did you handle it?

_____
_____
_____
_____
_____
_____
_____
_____
_____

What was the outcome?

_____

_____

_____

_____

_____

_____

_____

_____

_____

What could you have done differently?

_____

_____

_____

_____

_____

_____

_____

_____

_____

Notes

FAMILY

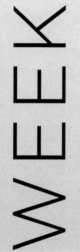

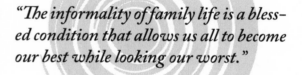

*"The informality of family life is a bless-
ed condition that allows us all to become
our best while looking our worst."*

~ Marge Kennedy

Focus on *Family*

Connection makes us human. Our relationships enrich our lives in so many ways. What relationships would you like to expand?

_____

_____

_____

_____

_____

What can you do to facilitate it?

_____

_____

_____

_____

_____

_____

_____

_____

_____

_____

_____

_____

I will connect with those I love in these three ways:

_____

_____

_____

_____

_____

_____

_____

_____

_____

_____

_____

_____

_____

_____

_____

_____

_____

_____

Notes

LEADERSHIP

WEEK 10

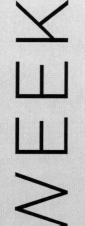

"Fight for the things that you care about. But do it in a way that will lead others to join you."

~ Ruth Bader Ginsberg

Focus on *Leadership*

What are you passionate about that would compel you to inspire others?

_____

_____

_____

_____

_____

_____

_____

_____

_____

_____

If you are not already doing so, what can you do to incorporate these into your life now?

_____

_____

_____

_____

_____

_____

_____

How will you choose to lead?

_____

_____

_____

_____

_____

_____

_____

_____

_____

Notes

LEGACY

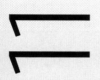

WEEK 11

"There is no greater agony than bearing an untold story inside you."

~ Maya Angelou,
I Know Why the Caged Bird Sings

Focus on *Legacy*

What do you still want to accomplish? What else do you want to share with the world?

_____

_____

_____

_____

_____

_____

_____

_____

_____

How will this impact the world?

_____

_____

_____

_____

_____

_____

_____

_____

_____

What is your legacy?

_____
_____
_____
_____
_____
_____
_____
_____

Why is this important to you?

_____
_____
_____
_____
_____
_____
_____
_____

Notes

HEALTH

WEEK 12

"Keep your vitality. A life without health is like a river without water."

~ Maxime Lagacé

Focus on *Health*

What makes your body feel good?

_____

_____

_____

_____

_____

_____

_____

_____

_____

_____

_____

What's your favorite exercise?

_____

_____

_____

_____

_____

_____

What do you eat that makes you feel awake and alert?

_____

_____

_____

_____

_____

_____

_____

_____

_____

_____

_____

_____

_____

_____

_____

_____

_____

_____

_____

_____

Notes

TIME

WEEK 13

"Time is money."

~ Benjamin Franklin

Focus on *Time*

How do you spend your time?

_____
_____
_____
_____
_____
_____
_____
_____
_____

What do you do to waste time?

_____
_____
_____
_____
_____
_____
_____
_____
_____

What would you like to do instead?

_____

_____

_____

_____

_____

_____

_____

_____

_____

_____

Notes

SPHERE OF SUPPORT

WEEK 14

"Surround yourself with people who make you happy. People who make you laugh, who help you when you're in need. People who genuinely care. They are the ones worth keeping in your life. Everyone else is just passing through."

~ Karl Marx

Focus on *Relationships*

Who do you surround yourself with?

_____

_____

_____

_____

_____

_____

_____

_____

_____

_____

_____

_____

_____

_____

_____

_____

_____

_____

Why?

_____

_____

_____

_____

_____

_____

_____

_____

Who else do you want in your life?

_____

_____

_____

_____

_____

_____

_____

_____

Notes

Empowerment

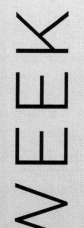

"Power can be taken, but not given. The process of the taking is empowerment in itself."

~ Gloria Steinem

Focus on *Empowerment*

Do you own your own power and feed it with positivity?

Circle one: YES *or* NO

What can you do differently to support yourself? How about daily exercise, good food habits or meditation? Write down three ideas here:

1. _____

_____

_____

_____

2. _____

_____

_____

_____

3. _____

_____

_____

_____

Do you surround yourself with people that empower you to be your best self?

Circle one: YES *or* NO

If NO, *pick three people you know that empower you who you want to spend more time with:*

1.
_____

2.
_____

3.
_____

If YES, pick three more people who will also empower you or will empower you even more:

1.
_____

2.
_____

3.
_____

Notes

OPPORTUNITIES

16

WEEK

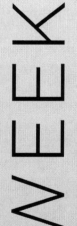

"When one door of happiness closes, another opens; but often we look so long at the closed door that we do not see the one which has been opened for us."

~ Helen Keller

Focus on *Opportunities*

What opportunities are available to you right now?

_____

_____

_____

_____

_____

_____

_____

_____

Perhaps people or ideas or offers that you haven't paid attention to?

_____

_____

_____

_____

_____

_____

_____

_____

Perhaps ones where you haven't properly considered all the pros and cons?

_____

_____

_____

_____

_____

_____

_____

What have you missed or maybe not previously seen?

_____

_____

_____

_____

_____

_____

_____

_____

_____

Notes

ALIGNMENT

WEEK 17

"When the basis for your actions is inner alignment with the present moment, your actions become empowered by the intelligence of life itself."

~Eckhart Tolle

Focus on *Alignment*

Is what you're doing right now aligned with your best self?

_____

_____

_____

_____

_____

_____

_____

_____

_____

_____

_____

_____

_____

_____

_____

_____

_____

_____

_____

_____

_____

What do you do that supports your alignment with your best self?

_____

_____

_____

_____

_____

_____

_____

_____

_____

What can you do differently to support your alignment in more positive ways?

_____

_____

_____

_____

_____

_____

_____

_____

Notes

KNOWLEDGE

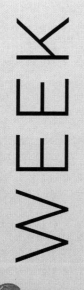

WEEK 18

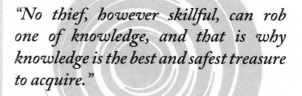

"No thief, however skillful, can rob one of knowledge, and that is why knowledge is the best and safest treasure to acquire."

~ L. Frank Baum
The Lost Princess of Oz

Focus on *Knowledge*

What have you learned that has helped you the most?

_____

_____

_____

_____

_____

_____

_____

_____

_____

_____

_____

_____

_____

_____

_____

How did you apply it?

Focus on *Knowledge*

Who did you learn it from? Have you thanked them?

_____

_____

_____

_____

_____

_____

_____

_____

_____

_____

_____

_____

_____

_____

_____

_____

_____

_____

_____

Was it easy to learn? Why?

Notes

PERMISSION

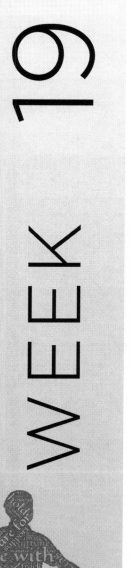

WEEK 19

"When you give yourself permission to communicate what matters to you in every situation you will have peace despite rejection or disapproval. Putting a voice to your soul helps you to let go of the negative energy of fear and regret."

~ Shannon L. Alder

Focus on *Permission*

What do you ask yourself permission for that doesn't require it?

_____

_____

_____

_____

_____

_____

_____

_____

_____

_____

_____

_____

_____

_____

_____

_____

_____

_____

_____

What would you need to do to give yourself permission? When will you do that?

_____

_____

_____

_____

_____

_____

_____

_____

_____

_____

_____

_____

_____

_____

_____

_____

_____

_____

_____

Notes

MAGIC

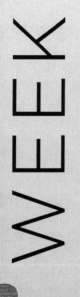

WEEK 20

"*And above all, watch with glittering eyes the whole world around you because the greatest secrets are always hidden in the most unlikely places. Those who don't believe in magic will never find it.*"

– *Roald Dahl*

Focus on *Magic*

If you could press a magic button and be anyone, who would you want to be? Why?

_____

_____

_____

_____

_____

_____

_____

_____

_____

_____

_____

_____

_____

_____

_____

_____

_____

What are the characteristics of that person?

_____

_____

_____

_____

_____

_____

_____

_____

_____

_____

_____

_____

_____

_____

_____

_____

_____

_____

Notes

NEW BEGINNINGS

WEEK 21

"The beginning is always today."

– Mary Shelley

Focus on *New Beginnings*

If you could start all over, what would you do for a living?

_____

_____

_____

_____

_____

_____

_____

_____

_____

_____

_____

_____

_____

_____

_____

_____

_____

_____

_____

_____

_____

_____

_____

_____

_____

_____

_____

_____

_____

_____

_____

_____

_____

_____

_____

_____

_____

_____

_____

_____

Notes

ADAPTABILITY

WEEK 22

"It is not the strongest or the most intelligent who will survive but those who can best manage change."

~ Leon C. Megginson

Focus on *Adapting*

Are you adaptable? If yes, why?

_____

_____

_____

_____

_____

_____

_____

_____

_____

_____

_____

_____

_____

_____

_____

_____

_____

If no, what's blocking you?

_____
_____
_____
_____
_____
_____
_____
_____
_____
_____
_____
_____
_____
_____
_____
_____
_____

Notes

TRAVEL

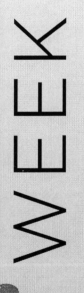

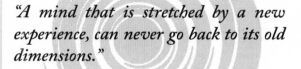

"A mind that is stretched by a new experience, can never go back to its old dimensions."

~ Oliver Wendell Holmes

Focus on *Travel*

Travel changes us. It is an amazing opportunity to learn and grow. Where would you like to go?

These are three places I will visit this year:

_____

_____

_____

_____

_____

_____

_____

_____

_____

_____

_____

_____

_____

_____

_____

_____

_____

_____

Notes

HABITS

"*The chains of habit are too weak to be felt until they are too strong to be broken.*"

— *Samuel Johnson*

Focus on *Habits*

List your good habits:

_____

_____

_____

_____

_____

_____

_____

_____

_____

_____

List your bad habits

_____

_____

_____

_____

_____

_____

_____

_____

_____

_____

Which habits serve your higher self?

_____

_____

_____

_____

_____

_____

_____

_____

_____

Which habits do you want to change?

_____

_____

_____

_____

_____

_____

_____

_____

_____

Notes

PRACTICE MAKES PERFECT

"It is a mistake to think that the practice of my art has become easy to me. I assure you, dear friend, no one has given so much care to the study of composition as I. There is scarcely a famous master in music whose works I have not frequently and diligently studied."

~Wolfgang Amadeus Mozart

Focus on *Practicing*

What do you need to keep practicing?
(Choose at least 2 and write them down here)

_____

_____

_____

_____

_____

_____

_____

_____

_____

_____

_____

_____

_____

_____

_____

_____

_____

_____

_____

_____

_____

_____

_____

_____

_____

_____

_____

_____

_____

_____

_____

_____

_____

_____

_____

_____

_____

Notes

LIVE

WEEK 26

"You've gotta dance like there's nobody watching, love like you'll never be hurt, sing like there's nobody listening, And live like it's heaven on earth."

~William W. Purkey

Focus on *Living*

What have you not done that you wish you would have done?

_____

_____

_____

_____

_____

_____

_____

_____

_____

_____

_____

_____

_____

_____

_____

_____

_____

_____

_____

When will you do it? Write down a date for each idea that you wrote down.

_____

_____

_____

_____

_____

_____

_____

_____

_____

_____

_____

_____

_____

_____

_____

_____

_____

_____

_____

Notes

CHANGE

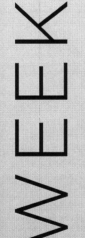

WEEK 27

"Be the change that you wish to see in the world."

~ Mahatma Gandhi

Focus on *Change*

What do you see around you that you would like to change?

_____

_____

_____

_____

_____

_____

_____

_____

_____

_____

_____

_____

_____

_____

_____

_____

_____

_____

_____

What can you do to contribute to that change?

Notes

CELEBRATION

WEEK 28

"Without music, life would be a mistake."

~ Friedrich Nietzsche,
Twilight of the Idols

Focus on *Celebration*

Can you make time today to dance and sing?
Circle one: YES or NO?

Do you have a "Celebration" playlist? If so,
when do you listen to that playlist? If not,
what's stopping you?

_____

_____

_____

_____

_____

_____

Make one now. Start with five songs that
make you feel good.

1. _____
2. _____
3. _____
4. _____
5. _____

Add five more songs now

6. _____

7. _____

8. _____

9. _____

10. _____

What are you dancing to now?

_____

_____

_____

What else can you do to celebrate you and your wins?

_____

_____

_____

_____

_____

_____

_____

Notes

UNBURDEN YOURSELF

WEEK 29

"Faith is to believe what you do not see; the reward of this faith is to see what you believe."

~ Saint Augustine

Focus on *Letting Go*

What are you carrying that you can give to your higher power?

_____

_____

_____

_____

_____

_____

_____

_____

_____

_____

_____

_____

_____

_____

_____

_____

_____

_____

_____

Notes

MIRACLES

WEEK 30

"There are only two ways to live your life. One is as though nothing is a miracle. The other is as though everything is a miracle."

~ Albert Einstein

Focus on *Miracles*

What miracles are you grateful for?

What are some miracles you might have missed?

_____

_____

_____

_____

_____

_____

_____

_____

_____

_____

_____

_____

_____

_____

_____

_____

Will you make it a practice to keep your eyes open for more miracles? Circle: YES or NO

Notes

THE GIFT

"Yesterday is history, tomorrow is a mystery, today is a gift of God, which is why we call it the present."

~ Bill Keane

Focus on *Your Life*

Where do you spend most of your time—past, present or future—and why?

_____

_____

_____

_____

_____

_____

_____

_____

_____

_____

_____

_____

Where would you like to spend more time?

_____

_____

_____

_____

How will that make your life better?

_____

_____

_____

_____

_____

_____

_____

_____

_____

_____

_____

_____

_____

_____

_____

_____

_____

Notes

ANGER

"Speak when you are angry and you'll make the best speech you'll ever regret."

~ Laurence J. Peter

Focus on *Making Amends*

Is there anyone that you have spoken to in anger that you still need to apologize to?

_____

_____

_____

_____

_____

_____

_____

_____

_____

_____

_____

_____

_____

_____

_____

_____

_____

_____

_____

_____

What can you do to apologize to them today so you can move on now?

_____

_____

_____

_____

_____

_____

_____

_____

_____

_____

_____

_____

_____

_____

_____

_____

_____

_____

_____

_____

Notes

YOU

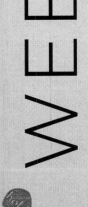

"Be yourself; everyone else is already taken."

~ Oscar Wilde

Focus on *You!*

List all the things you LOVE about yourself!

_____

_____

_____

_____

_____

_____

_____

_____

_____

_____

_____

_____

_____

_____

_____

_____

_____

_____

_____

_____

_____

_____

You are amazing! Keep going!

_____

_____

_____

_____

_____

_____

_____

_____

_____

_____

_____

_____

_____

_____

_____

_____

_____

_____

_____

Now Celebrate You!

Notes

PROGRESS

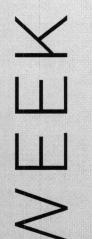

"People who spend most of their time in the present tend to be happiest. People who look to the future and learn from the past make the most progress."

~ Elysia Stobbe

Focus on *Progress*

What's the biggest lesson you have learned from your past?

_____
_____
_____
_____
_____
_____
_____

What have you done differently since then?

_____
_____
_____
_____
_____
_____
_____
_____
_____

How has that benefited you?

Notes

FAILING FORWARD

WEEK 35

"I have not failed. I've just found 10,000 ways that won't work."

~Thomas A. Edison

Learning from *Failure*

What is something that you failed at that you learned from?

_____

_____

_____

_____

_____

_____

_____

_____

_____

_____

_____

_____

_____

_____

_____

_____

_____

_____

_____

_____

How has that helped you today?

Notes

ENGAGE

WEEK 36

"The opposite of love is not hate, it's
indifference. The opposite of art is not
ugliness, it's indifference. The opposite
of faith is not heresy, it's indifference.
And the opposite of life is not death, it's
indifference."

~ Elie Wiesel

Focus on *Engagement*

What can you do to be more engaged in your life and with those around you?

List a few ways you can incorporate this into your daily life.

_____

_____

_____

_____

_____

_____

_____

_____

_____

_____

_____

_____

_____

_____

_____

_____

_____

_____

_____

Notes

YOUR JOURNEY

WEEK 37

"You have brains in your head. You have feet in your shoes. You can steer yourself any direction you choose. You're on your own. And you know what you know. And YOU are the one who'll decide where to go ..."

~ Dr. Seuss,
Oh, the Places You'll Go!

Focus on *Your Journey*

Are you happy with the path that you are traveling? Circle one: YES or NO

If YES, list all the amazing things you are happy about:

_____

_____

_____

_____

_____

_____

_____

_____

_____

_____

_____

_____

_____

_____

If not, what will you change today that will contribute to your happiness?

_____

_____

_____

_____

_____

_____

_____

What else can you do to increase your daily happiness?

_____

_____

_____

_____

_____

_____

_____

Notes

STORY

WEEK 38

"It's like everyone tells a story about themselves inside their own head. Always. All the time. That story makes you what you are. We build ourselves out of that story."

~ Patrick Rothfuss

Focus on *Your Story*

What's your story?

_____

_____

_____

_____

_____

_____

_____

_____

_____

_____

_____

_____

_____

_____

_____

_____

_____

_____

_____

_____

Does it strengthen or weaken you? Why?

_____

_____

_____

_____

_____

_____

_____

_____

_____

What can you change in your story?

_____

_____

_____

_____

_____

_____

_____

_____

Focus on *Your Story*

What needs to change in your story?

_____

_____

_____

_____

_____

_____

_____

_____

_____

_____

_____

_____

_____

_____

_____

_____

_____

_____

_____

_____

_____

What's your new story?

_____

_____

_____

_____

_____

_____

_____

_____

_____

_____

_____

_____

_____

_____

_____

_____

_____

_____

Notes

LOVE

WEEK 39

"You don't need to justify your love, you don't need to explain your love, you just need to practice your love. Practice creates the master."

~ Don Miguel Ruiz
The Mastery of Love: A Practical Guide to the Art of Relationship

Focus on *Love*

Who do you love? How do they make you feel?

_____

_____

_____

_____

_____

_____

_____

_____

_____

_____

_____

_____

_____

_____

_____

_____

_____

_____

_____

What's special about them?

_____

_____

_____

_____

_____

_____

_____

_____

_____

_____

_____

_____

_____

_____

_____

_____

_____

_____

_____

_____

_____

Focus on *Love*

Who loves you? How do they make you feel?

_____

_____

_____

_____

_____

_____

_____

What can you do to let them know you love them?

_____

_____

_____

_____

_____

What else can you do to let them know you love them?

_____

_____

_____

_____

_____

_____

_____

_____

_____

_____

When will you make it a habit to cherish those you love even more?

_____

_____

_____

Notes

SEX

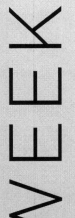

WEEK 40

"Sex, whatever else it is, is an athletic skill. The more you practice, the more you can, the more you want to, the more you enjoy it, the less it tires you."

~ Robert A. Heinlein
The Cat Who Walks Through Walls

Focus on *Sex*

What is wonderful about your sex life?

_____
_____
_____
_____
_____
_____
_____
_____

What is missing from your sex life?

_____
_____
_____
_____
_____
_____
_____
_____
_____
_____

What would you like to add to your sex life?

_____

_____

_____

_____

_____

_____

_____

_____

_____

_____

_____

_____

_____

_____

_____

_____

_____

_____

_____

Notes

DREAMS

"Everything you can imagine is real."

~ Pablo Picasso

Focus on *Your Dreams*

What is one thing you've always dreamed of doing or having or accomplishing that you just haven't gotten around to doing yet?

_____

_____

_____

_____

_____

_____

_____

_____

_____

_____

_____

_____

_____

How much longer until you make your dream a reality?

_____

_____

_____

What steps will you take now to make your dream a reality?

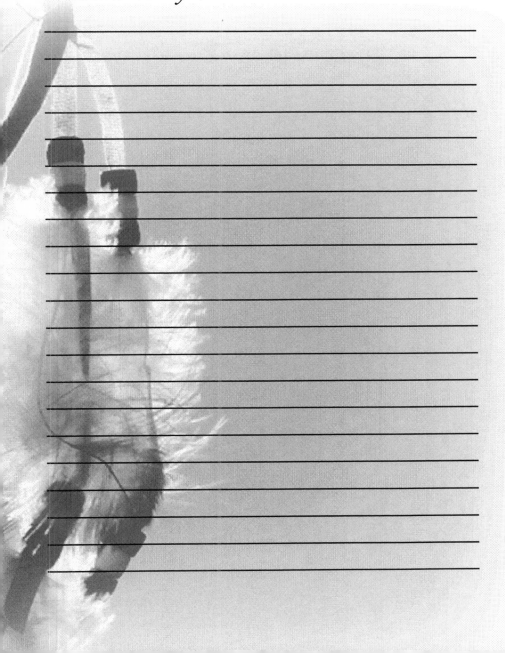

_____

_____

_____

_____

_____

_____

_____

_____

_____

_____

_____

_____

_____

_____

_____

_____

_____

_____

_____

_____

Notes

POTENTIAL

WEEK 42

"The big challenge is to become all that you have the possibility of becoming. You cannot believe what it does to the human spirit to maximize your human potential and stretch yourself to the limit."

~ Jim Rohn

Focus on *Potential*

Do you feel you are living up to your potential?

Circle one: YES or NO

If not, what is stopping you from reaching your full potential?

If yes, why and what can you do to keep supporting yourself and moving forward?

_____

_____

_____

_____

_____

_____

_____

_____

_____

_____

_____

What small changes can you make right now that will move you closer to being your best self?

_____

_____

_____

_____

_____

_____

_____

_____

_____

What big changes will you make?

_____

_____

_____

_____

_____

_____

_____

_____

_____

Focus on *Potential*

What needs to happen for you to reach peak performance?

_____

_____

_____

_____

_____

_____

_____

_____

_____

Why is this important to you?

_____

_____

_____

_____

_____

_____

_____

_____

_____

How will this impact your life?

_____

_____

_____

_____

_____

_____

_____

_____

_____

_____

_____

When will you make these changes?

_____

_____

_____

_____

_____

_____

Notes

ACTION

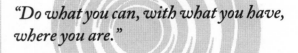

"Do what you can, with what you have, where you are."

~ Theodore Roosevelt

Focus on *Action*

What will you act on today that you meant to in the past, but didn't? Choose at least two things and write them down.

_____

_____

_____

_____

_____

_____

_____

_____

_____

_____

_____

_____

_____

_____

_____

_____

_____

_____

What will you do this time to ensure that you take action?

_____

_____

_____

_____

_____

_____

_____

How will these actions benefit you?

_____

_____

_____

_____

_____

_____

_____

Focus on *Action*

Why are these actions important to you now?

_____

_____

_____

_____

_____

_____

_____

_____

_____

_____

_____

_____

_____

_____

_____

_____

_____

When will you fulfill these promises to yourself? Write down a date for each one you chose.

_____

_____

_____

_____

_____

_____

_____

_____

_____

_____

_____

_____

_____

_____

_____

_____

_____

_____

Notes

REGRETS

WEEK 44

"*I made decisions that I regret and I took them as learning experiences. I'm human, not perfect, like anybody else.*"

~ Queen Latifah

Learning from *Regret*

What regrets do you have that you can change to learning lessons instead?

_____

_____

_____

_____

_____

_____

_____

_____

_____

_____

_____

_____

_____

_____

_____

_____

What regrets do you have that you want to release? Write them down and let them go now.

_____

_____

_____

_____

_____

_____

_____

_____

_____

_____

_____

_____

_____

_____

_____

_____

_____

_____

Notes

THANKFULNESS

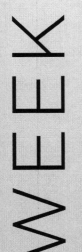

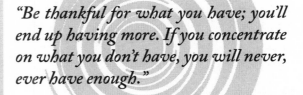

"Be thankful for what you have; you'll end up having more. If you concentrate on what you don't have, you will never, ever have enough."

~ Oprah Winfrey

Elysia Stobbe

Focus on *Thankfulness*

What could you be thankful for today that you let slip by?

_____

_____

_____

_____

_____

_____

_____

_____

What could you be thankful for this week that you missed?

_____

_____

_____

_____

_____

_____

_____

_____

What can you do in the future to show appreciation for the people you are thankful for in your life?

_____

_____

_____

_____

_____

_____

_____

_____

_____

_____

_____

_____

_____

_____

_____

_____

_____

_____

Notes

ABUNDANCE

"*Acknowledging the good that you already have in your life is the foundation for all abundance.*"

~ Eckhart Tolle

Focus on *Abundance*

What is your cup overflowing with today? Choose at least three things you have that someone else does not.

How can you share your abundance with others?

Notes

YOUR THOUGHTS

WEEK 47

"Your beliefs become your thoughts,
Your thoughts become your words,
Your words become your actions,
Your actions become your habits,
Your habits become your values,
Your values become your destiny."

~ Mahatma Gandhi

Focus on *Thoughts*

I have the quote from the previous page as one of the rotating screensavers on my computer. It's a great reminder for me that what I think ultimately becomes my destiny whether those thoughts are conscious or unconscious.

What would you like your destiny to be?

_____
_____
_____
_____
_____
_____
_____
_____
_____
_____
_____
_____

Do you pay attention to your thoughts?
Circle YES or NO

If they are negative thoughts, do you stop them
and course correct? Circle YES or NO

If they are positive thoughts, do you focus more
on them? Circle YES or NO

What would you like to do differently to change
the outcome of your destiny?

Notes

INVEST IN YOU

WEEK 48

"The key is in not spending time, but in investing it."

~ Stephen R. Covey

Your time is *Valuable*

Where do you waste time? Pick three specific examples, it can be daily or weekly.

_____

_____

_____

_____

_____

_____

_____

_____

_____

_____

_____

_____

_____

_____

What could you do instead with that time?
Choose three things you can do with that time
to invest in yourself.

_____

_____

_____

_____

_____

_____

_____

What will you commit to doing to make that
change happen now?

_____

_____

_____

_____

_____

_____

Notes

BE PRESENT

WEEK 49

"Time is free, but it's priceless. You can't own it, but you can use it. You can't keep it, but you can spend it. Once you've lost it you can never get it back."

~ Harvey Mackay

Focus on *Being Present*

I am very particular about who I choose to spend time with. When I am with those I care about and do choose to spend time with, I do my best to be fully present.

What does that mean? I am actively listening and engaged with them. I want them to know that they are important to me. What does that look like? Well, for starters, I'm not checking my cell phone. In fact, most of the time if I am at dinner, it's not even on the table or anywhere I can see it.

When I look around a restaurant and see couples on their cell phones instead of actively engaged with one another, it saddens me. They are letting the most precious commodity of time slip through their fingers and missing the wonderful opportunity to show someone they care about that that person matters to them. But this is only one example.

How many of us act like we are listening when we're really thinking about something else? Are you giving that person your full attention? I know we all can work on that one!

How often are you truly present in the moment? Be honest with yourself.

_____

_____

_____

Why? What else are you thinking about?

_____

_____

_____

_____

_____

What joys have you missed by not being present?

_____

_____

_____

_____

_____

Focus on *Being Present*

Who have you hurt by not being present in the moment?

_____

_____

_____

_____

_____

_____

_____

What will you change about how you spend time with people from now on?

_____

_____

_____

_____

_____

_____

_____

How will that benefit the people you care about?

_____

_____

_____

_____

_____

_____

_____

_____

How will that benefit you?

_____

_____

_____

_____

_____

_____

_____

_____

_____

Notes

WORK

WEEK 50

" *The purpose of life is to discover your gift. The work of life is to develop it. The meaning of life is to give your gift away.*"

~ David Viscott

Focus on *Work*

What are you working on that excites you?

_____

_____

_____

_____

_____

_____

_____

_____

_____

What are you working on that will help you reach your full potential?

_____

_____

_____

_____

_____

_____

_____

_____

_____

What are you working on that you can delegate?

_____

_____

_____

_____

_____

_____

_____

_____

How will you make that happen?

_____

_____

_____

_____

_____

_____

_____

Focus on *Work*

When will you delegate it? _____

Would now be a good time? _____

Now that you've gotten that off your plate, how will that positively impact your goals?

_____

_____

_____

_____

_____

_____

What can you do to turn your work into play?

_____

_____

_____

_____

_____

_____

_____

_____

_____

What can you do to turn your work into your passion?

_____

_____

_____

_____

_____

_____

_____

_____

_____

What are you passionate about that you can turn into a career or a business?

_____

_____

_____

_____

_____

_____

_____

_____

_____

Notes

COMPASSION

WEEK 51

"Compassion is born from understanding suffering. We all should learn to embrace our own suffering, to listen to it deeply, and to have a deep look into its nature."

~ Thich Nhat Hanh
The Art of Communicating

Focus on *Compassion*

Are you able to feel compassion for others? Cirle YES or NO

Are you able to show others compassion?

Circle YES or NO

Are you able to give yourself the gift of compassion? Circle YES or NO

Is there anything you would like to do differently and more compassionately?

_____

_____

_____

_____

_____

_____

_____

_____

_____

_____

_____

_____

Notes

WISDOM

WEEK 52

"*Knowing yourself is the beginning of all wisdom.*"

~ Aristotle

Focus on *Wisdom*

When you know yourself there is an elevated awareness of a variety of types of wisdom.

Here are a few types of wisdom you have gained through the processes in this book: intuitive, intellectual, spiritual and self.

What other types of wisdom do you possess?

_____

_____

_____

_____

_____

_____

_____

_____

_____

_____

_____

_____

When you are in tune with these various types of wisdom, how does it add to your life?

_____

_____

_____

_____

_____

_____

_____

_____

_____

_____

_____

_____

_____

_____

_____

_____

_____

_____

Focus on *Wisdom*

What other types of wisdom do you want?

_____

_____

_____

_____

_____

_____

_____

_____

_____

_____

_____

_____

_____

_____

_____

_____

_____

_____

_____

_____

_____

What steps can you take to add those additional types of wisdom?

_____

_____

_____

_____

_____

_____

_____

_____

_____

_____

_____

_____

_____

_____

_____

_____

_____

About the Author

Elysia Stobbe is the #1 Best Selling Author
of "How to Get Approved for the Best
Mortgage Without Sticking a Fork in Your
Eye ™"

As one of the nation's leading mortgage
experts with more than 18 years of
experience, Elysia has been featured in the
Wall Street Journal, on the Wall Street
Business Radio Network, NPR and on FOX,
ABC, NBC, CBS and more for her expertise
with mortgages and finance. In addition,
Elysia has been interviewed for U.S. News
& World Report multiple times as well as the National Association of
Realtors for Realtor.Com.

Elysia has also contributed to Zillow and RealEstate.com as well as The
American Business Journals, Apartment Therapy and I-95 Business.

Elysia has presented her "Secrets of Success" and "Managing Yourself &
Leading Others" at Harvard University. She's a national keynote speaker
on a variety of topics including financial freedom, home buying, residential
mortgages, wealth accumulation and strategic business coaching. In
addition to being a #1 best-selling author Elysia has served as a special
subject consultant to The New Oxford American Dictionary and also
contributed to "199 Facts About Credit Scores."

A few of Elysia's hobbies include travel, art, music, scuba diving, paddle
boarding and running, as well as constant and never-ending improvement.
Elysia has studied with Tony Robbins, Keith Cunningham and Dean
Grasiosi.

Visit ElysiaStobbeInc.com for more information. For other books by
Elysia, visit ElysiaStobbeBooks.com